Boys Big Book of Holiday Fun

Travel Time For Kids

Fantastic fun for children
aged 6 and over.

HAPPY DAYS

Use this page to help record the best bits of your holidays.

Date: _____

Today I visited: _____

_____

People who came with me:

_____

_____

Stick your ticket here.

Weather: ☐ 🙂 ☐ 🌧 ☐ 🌦 ☐ ❄ ☐ ⛈

Best part: _____ Score: __/10

Other good bits: _____

_____

I ate: _____

I played: _____

_____

Today was:

☐ Simply awesome   ☐ Just brilliant
☐ Good fun   ☐ Quite a laugh
☐ Not bad   ☐ Disappointing

Draw a picture or paste a photo here.

WATERWORLD

Can you guide Roberto through the splash park maze to reach the beach at the bottom?

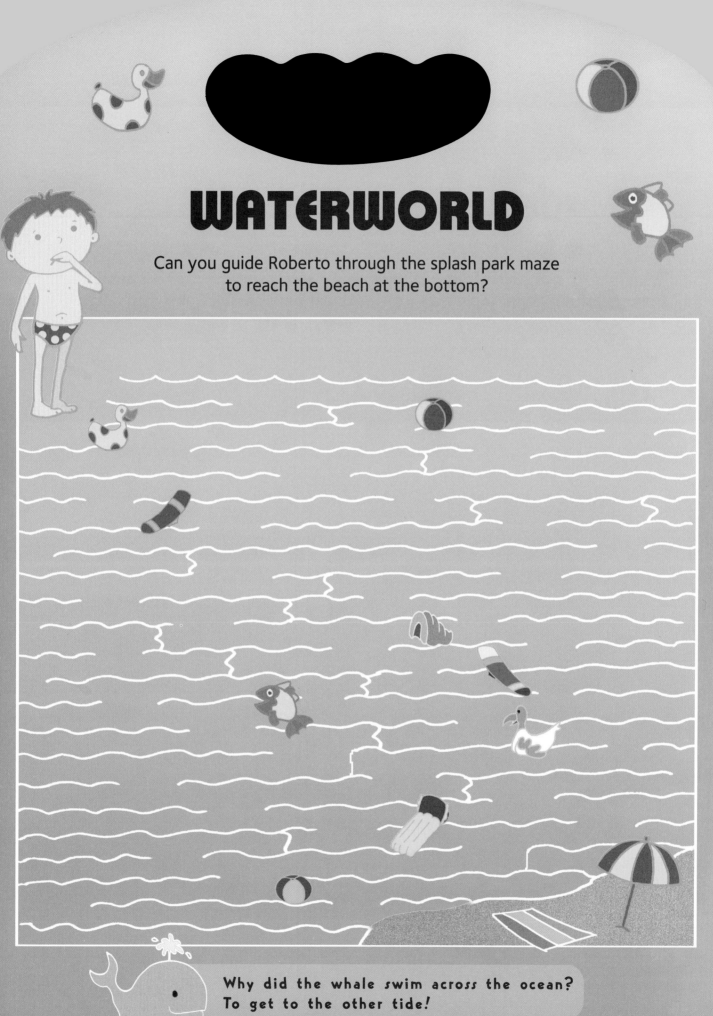

Why did the whale swim across the ocean?
To get to the other tide!

TRAVEL BINGO

This is a terrific game when travelling and you will need two players and two pencils. The aim is to spot each of the 12 items on the game card (below). As soon as you spot one of the items, put a tick in the relevant box. The first player to tick all 12 boxes is a Bingo winner! Player 1 ticks the grey box, and player 2 ticks the white box.

Where do cows go on holiday?
Moo York!

WHICH SANDWICH?

Use your brain power to work out which sandwich Harry wants in his picnic basket.

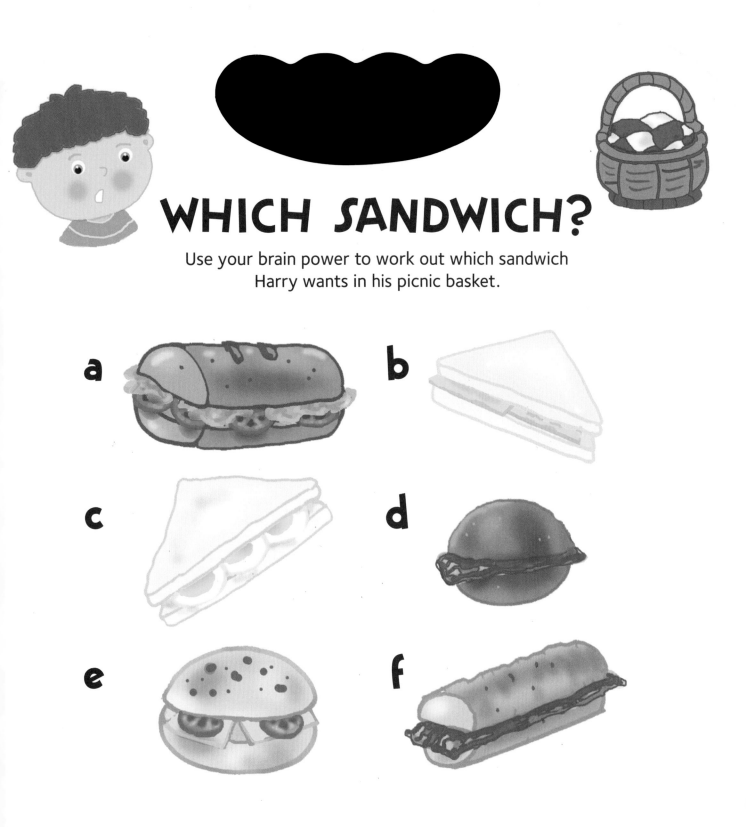

a

b

c

d

e

f

He doesn't want a crusty French stick sandwich.
He's not in the mood for a bacon bun.
Harry doesn't like tomatoes.
Egg sandwiches are too smelly!

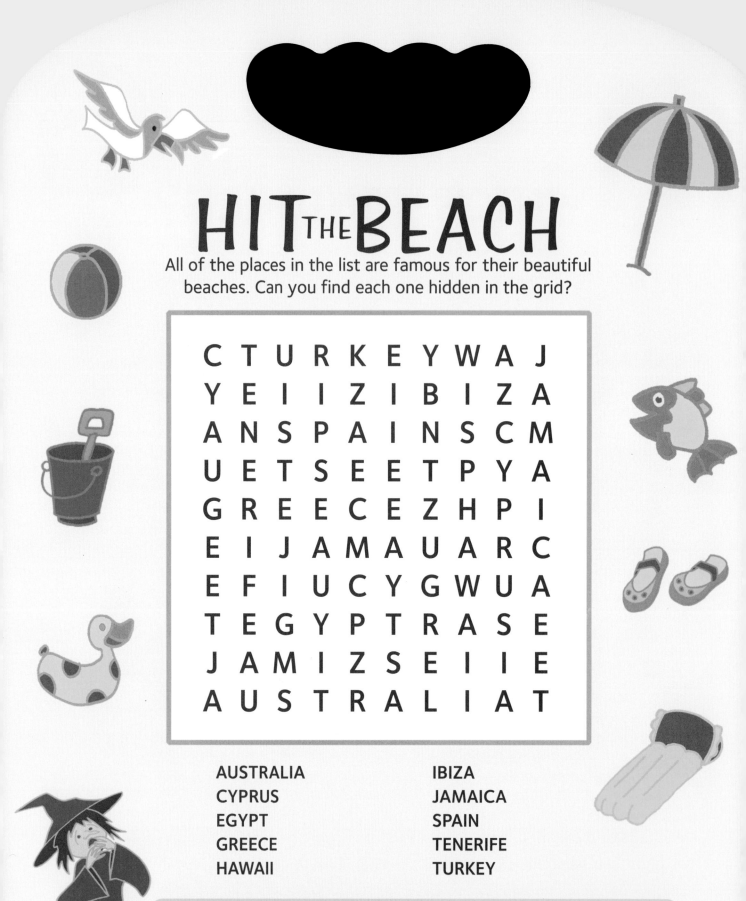

HIT THE BEACH

All of the places in the list are famous for their beautiful beaches. Can you find each one hidden in the grid?

```
C T U R K E Y W A J
Y E I I Z I B I Z A
A N S P A I N S C M
U E T S E E T P Y A
G R E E C E Z H P I
E I J A M A U A R C
E F I U C Y G W U A
T E G Y P T R A S E
J A M I Z S E I I E
A U S T R A L I A T
```

AUSTRALIA
CYPRUS
EGYPT
GREECE
HAWAII

IBIZA
JAMAICA
SPAIN
TENERIFE
TURKEY

What do you call a witch who's afraid of the beach?
A chicken sand-witch!

AROUND THE WORLD

Write the listed countries in the spiral so they all fit correctly.
Three letters are there already to help you.

When you've finished, use the letters in the dark green boxes to spell the largest country in the world.

ARGENTINA
AUSTRALIA
AUSTRIA
DENMARK
KENYA
NEW ZEALAND
PAKISTAN

The dark squares are the first letter of one country name and the last letter of another.

What stays in the corner but travels around the world?

A postage stamp!

HOLiDAY FORTUNES

Make a fortune teller to see what your holiday holds in store for you!

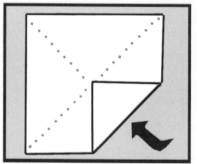

1. Cut a square of paper about the same size as the square on the opposite page. Draw lines diagonally from corner to corner, as shown above. Fold one corner so the point touches where the lines cross.

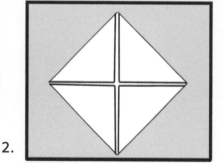

2. Fold the other three corners in the same way.

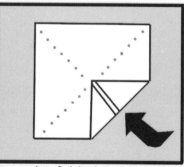

3. Turn the folded square over. Draw lines diagonally from corner to corner as you did before. Fold the corners so the points touch where the lines cross.

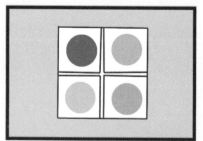

4. Turn the folded square over again. This is what it should look like. Colour a large dot on each quarter, as shown.

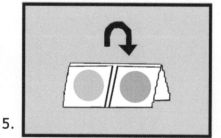

5. Fold in half, as shown, and unfold. Fold in half the other way and unfold.

6. Turn the folded square over again. Number the flaps from 1 to 8, as shown.

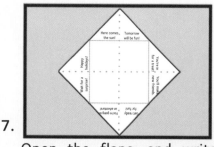

7. Open the flaps, and write mottoes like those on the page opposite. Close the flaps to see the numbers.

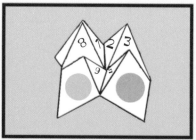

8. Turn over the square to see the coloured circles. Slot thumbs and 4th fingers into the corner pockets, and hold the fortune teller with the coloured circles facing up.

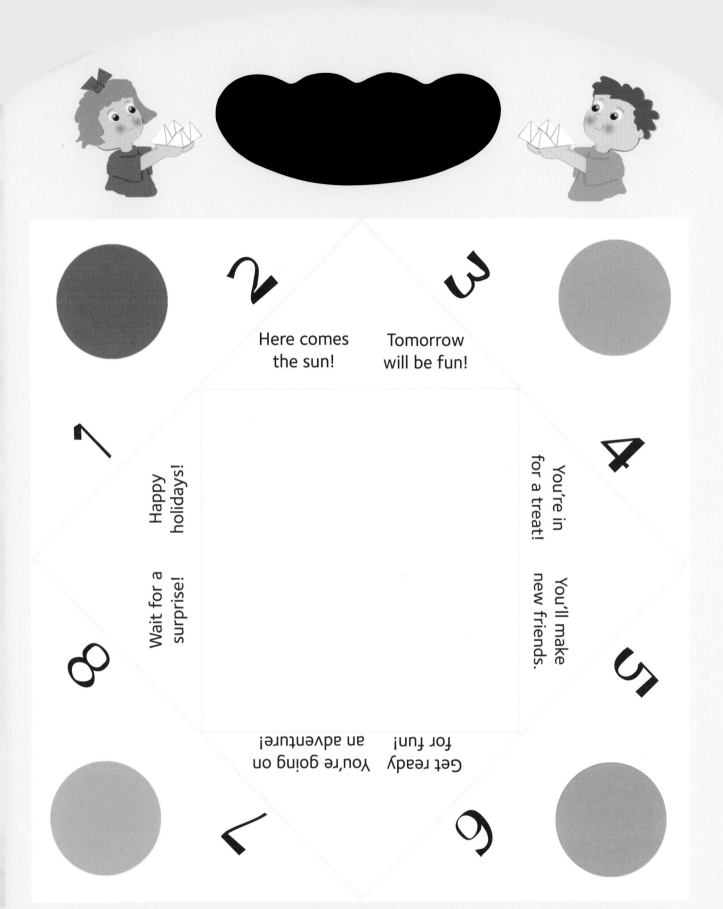

2 Here comes the sun!

3 Tomorrow will be fun!

1 Happy holidays!

4 You're in for a treat!

8 Wait for a surprise!

5 You'll make new friends.

7 You're going on an adventure!

6 Get ready for fun!

Now, you're ready to play. Ask a friend to choose a colour. Open and close the fortune teller the same number of times as there are letters in the colour word (RED = 3, for example). On the last 'letter', hold the fortune teller open and ask your friend to choose a number from the four revealed. Open and close the fortune teller that number of times. Hold the last position so your friend can choose a number. This time, open the flap for the chosen number and read the motto.

BRAIN-BUSTING QUIZ

How much do you know about the world?
Try this quiz to pass some time while you travel.

1. What is the capital city of France?

a. London   b. New York
c. Paris   d. Lyons

2. Florida is part of which country?
a. Canada   b. Jamaica
c. USA   d. Spain

3. Which country is this?

a. Australia   b. Mexico
c. Japan   d. Italy

4. What money would you spend in Spain?
a. dollars   b. euros
c. pounds   d. pesetas

5. What is this statue called?
The Statue of...

a. Freedom   b. Justice
c. Welcome   d. Liberty

6. Where would you go to sunbathe on the Algarve?
a. Menorca   b. Ibiza
c. Portugal   d. Barbados

7. Which continent is famous for its wildlife safaris?

a. Africa b. Europe
c. Asia d. South America

8. Which country has Ottawa as its capital city?
a. Canada b. Australia
c. Wales d. India

9. Where would you go to see these famous landmarks?

10. Which of these countries is NOT in Scandinavia?
a. Finland b. Sweden
c. Romania d. Norway

11. In which country could you visit the Great Barrier Reef?

a. Cuba b. Australia
c. Portugal d. South Africa

12. Which ocean separates Europe and the USA?
a. Atlantic b. Pacific
c. Indian d. Arctic

a. Brazil b. New Zealand
c. China d. Egypt

SHoW-SToPPeR

Ten things are different in the bottom picture. Can you circle them all?

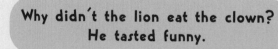

Why didn't the lion eat the clown?
He tasted funny.

12

TICKETS, PLEASE

These tickets have been torn by accident.
Can you match the halves so they spell the names of places?

rife

dam

Tene

lulu

Istan

Johann

Amster

bul

What is the most dangerous city?

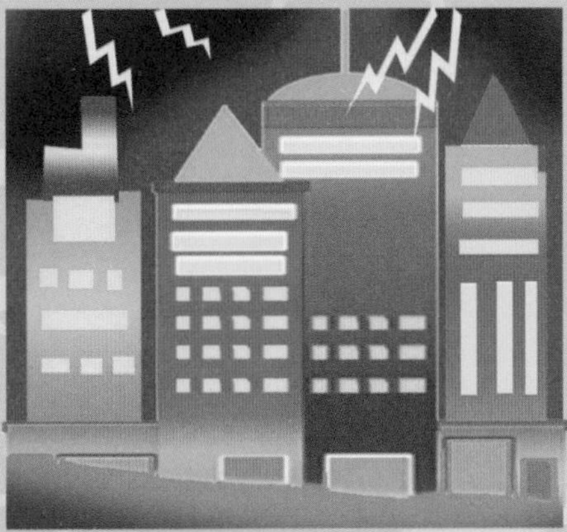

esburg

Hono

Electri-city!

FLYING HIGH

Add up the numbers on each kite tail to see which kite flies the highest.

Highest total wins.

What kind of clothes
do clouds wear?

Thunderwear!

PICTURE POSTCARD

Design and write your own postcard and then cut it out to send to someone back home! Draw a picture of the things you've done or a place you've seen on your holiday.

WE'RE HAVING FUN!

What did the postcard say to the stamp? Stick with me and we'll go places!

DEAR

LOVE FROM

ON SAFARI

A safari holiday allows you to see some amazing animals.
Can you find the name of these ten animals in the grid?

```
L E L E C S R H I R
E L E P H A N T L H
O E A T E C H E B I
P E E Z E B R A A N
A L L S T E L E B O
R G I R A F F E H C
D S O L H C C G Y E
G I N I R H I I E R
H I P P O E G R N O
L E B A B O O N A S
```

BABOON   HYENA
ELEPHANT   LEOPARD
CHEETAH   LION
GIRAFFE   RHINOCEROS
HIPPO   ZEBRA

What do you get if you cross a lion with a hyena?
I don't know, but if it laughs you'd better join in!

ON YOUR BiKE

Which one of these motorbikes is not exactly the same as the others?

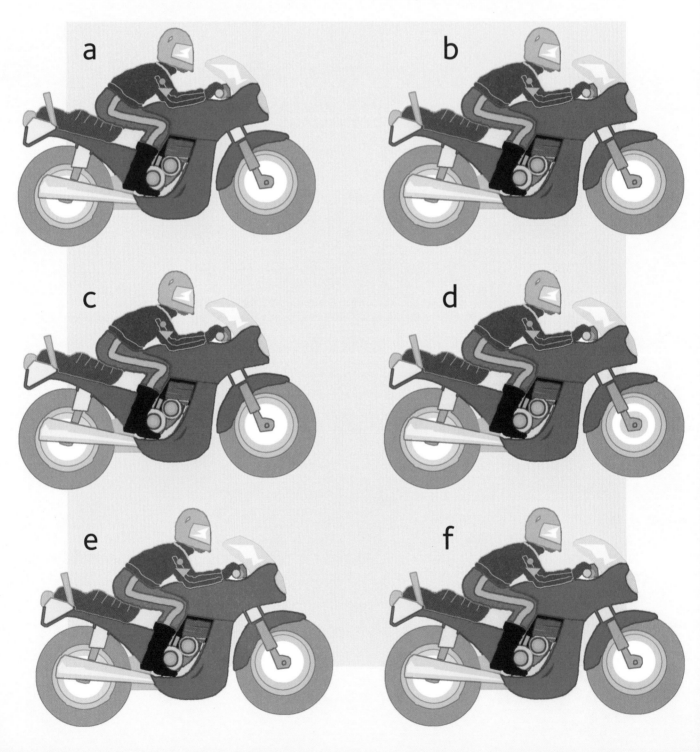

a

b

c

d

e

f

LOVELY LOLLIES

Find the correct path through the ice lollies and ice creams,
following the arrows in the right direction every time.

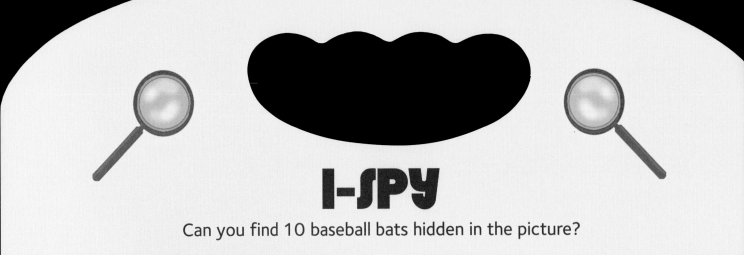

I-SPY

Can you find 10 baseball bats hidden in the picture?

ALL SQUARE

Play this game with two or three players. Each of you needs a pencil. When you've used this page, draw your own grid of dots on squared paper.

1 Player one draws a line to join two adjacent dots, either horizontally or vertically.

2 Player two does the same, anywhere on the grid.

3 Keep joining the dots until a player draws the fourth line to finish a square. The player writes his or her initials in the square to score one point.

4 Play until the grid is full, then count the initials to see which player has the most points.

TREASURE HUNT

Follow the clues to find where the treasure is buried.

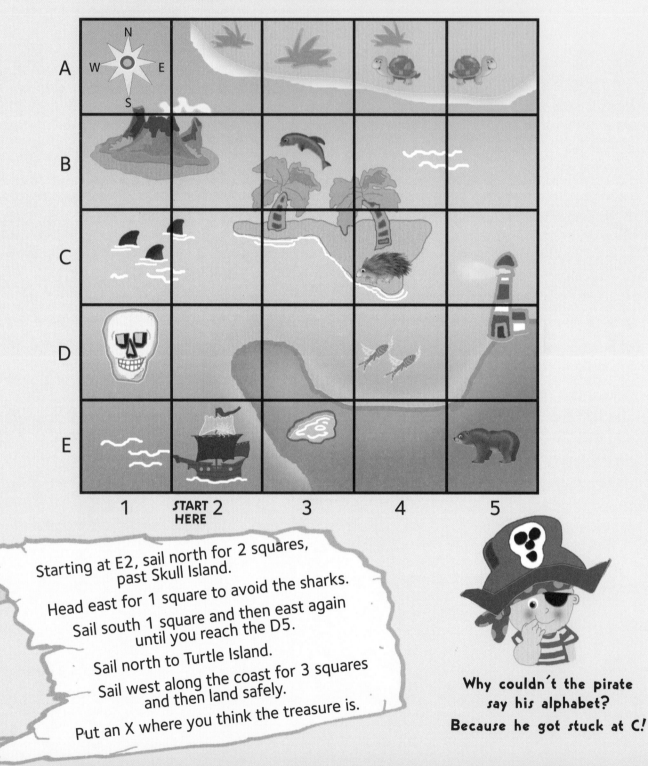

Starting at E2, sail north for 2 squares, past Skull Island.

Head east for 1 square to avoid the sharks.

Sail south 1 square and then east again until you reach the D5.

Sail north to Turtle Island.

Sail west along the coast for 3 squares and then land safely.

Put an X where you think the treasure is.

Why couldn't the pirate say his alphabet?

Because he got stuck at C!

HAPPY DAYS

Use this page to record the best bits of your holidays.

Date: _____

Today I visited: _____

_____

People who came with me:

_____

_____

Stick your ticket here.

Weather: 😊 ☁️ 🌧️ ❄️ ⛈️

Best part: _____ Score: /10

Other good bits: _____

_____

I ate: _____

I played: _____

_____

Today was:

☐ Simply awesome   ☐ Just brilliant

☐ Good fun   ☐ Quite a laugh

☐ Not bad   ☐ Disappointing

MARKET MAZE

Help the tourists find their way through the maze of streets and market stalls back to their cruise ship.

CHEQUERED FLAG

Motor racing is fast, furious and fun to watch!
Find all the motor sport words hidden in this grid.

H	W	H	A	I	R	P	I	N	X
A	C	W	W	H	E	E	L	D	M
M	O	H	D	Y	K	W	Z	R	E
E	C	E	R	I	N	D	C	S	C
C	K	P	I	T	S	T	O	P	H
H	P	I	V	B	E	F	M	O	A
I	I	N	E	R	E	L	E	I	N
C	T	D	R	A	L	A	C	L	I
B	R	A	K	E	S	G	H	E	C
F	L	I	N	D	Y	C	A	R	F

BRAKES INDYCAR
COCKPIT MECHANIC
DRIVER PITSTOP
FLAG SPOILER
HAIRPIN WHEEL

What kind of car does Luke Skywalker drive?
A Toy-yoda!

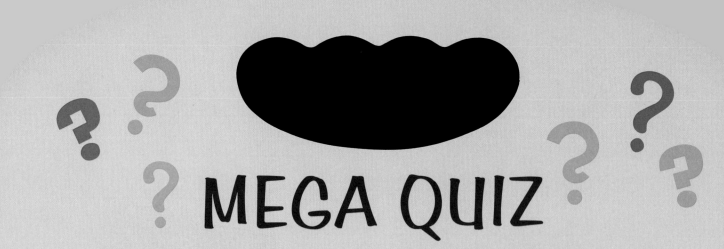

MEGA QUIZ

Are you feeling brainy? Try this travel quiz and see how many you get right.

1. Which of these travels the fastest?

a. family car   b. motorbike
c. jet plane   d. high-speed train

2. Which of these would be the best climate for a beach holiday?
a. temperate   b. tropical
c. arid   d. polar

3. How many travel pods are there on the London Eye?

a. 150   b. 300
c. 32   d. 6

4. "Bonjour" means "hello" in which language?
a. Spanish   b. Chinese
c. Swedish   d. French

5. The Taj Mahal is in which country?

a. India   b. China
c. Brazil   d. New Zealand

6. What's the name of Scooby Doo's vehicle?
a. The Crime Cruiser
b. The Riddle Rider
c. The Mystery Machine
d. The Vermillion Van

7. What title was given to an Ancient Egyptian ruler?
a. pharaoh   b. phoenix
c. phantom   d. phase

8. What is the name of the kingdom where Shrek lives?
a. Happy Ever After   b. Ogreville
c. Far Far Away   d. Grungedom

9. In which country would you find these creatures living in the wild?
a. South Africa   b. Australia
c. Scotland   d. Russia

10. Who uses the plane known as Air Force One?
a. Simon Cowell
b. David Beckham
c. The French president
d. The US president

11. Where do penguins live: near the North Pole or near the South Pole?

a. North Pole   b. South Pole

12. What do you call the throwing stick that should return to the person who threw it?
a. boomerang   b. catamaran
c. nickelodeon   d. didgeridoo

FRUIT-OKU

Solve the puzzle so that every row, column and mini-grid (four squares) has each of the four fruits in it.

JIG-FIT

Which of the five pieces could have come from the picture?

a   b   c   d   e

What did baby corn say to mummy corn?
Where's popcorn?

COUNTRY CONFUSION

Unscramble the names of the countries, and match each one to the correct postcard.

DINAI

INPSA

LAZERDTWINS

CEREGE

PAANJ

CAMAAJI

Which side of a moose is the furriest?

The outside!

FOUR IN A ROW

Here's a simple pen and paper game to pass the time on a long journey.
You need two players, each with a different coloured pen.

Player one colours a circle anywhere on the bottom row.

Player two takes his or her turn to colour a circle. This circle has to be next to the first circle so it can be on the bottom row, or in the row above player one's circle.

Players take turns to colour in a circle. Remember, a circle that has a blank circle below it cannot be coloured.

The first player to colour four in a row (across, down or diagonally) is the winner.

When you have used these two boards, draw your own on squared paper.

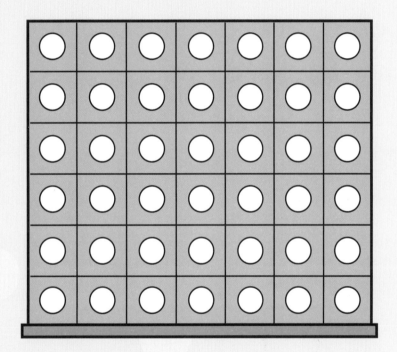

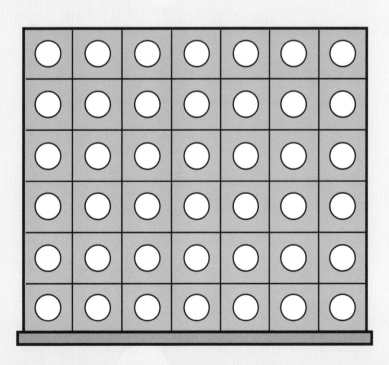

31

HAPPY DAYS

Use this page to record the best bits of your holidays.

Date: _____

Today I visited: _____

_____

People who came with me:

_____

_____

Stick your ticket here.

Weather: ☐ ☐ ☐ ☐ ☐

Best part: _____ Score: ___/10

Other good bits: _____

_____

I ate: _____

I played: _____

_____

Today was:

☐ Simply awesome   ☐ Just brilliant

☐ Good fun   ☐ Quite a laugh

☐ Not bad   ☐ Disappointing

Draw a picture or paste a photo here.

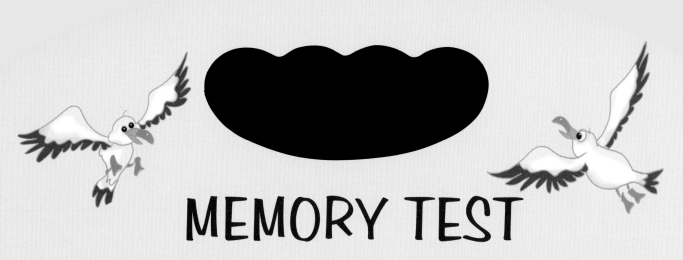

MEMORY TEST

Look carefully at this picture for a few minutes. Now turn the page and answer as many questions as you can. It's tricky!

MEMORY TEST

How many Memory Test picture questions can you answer correctly? No peeking!

1. How many yachts are there?
2. What colour towel is the girl holding?
3. What time is it?
4. What animal is on the beach?
5. What food can you buy at the snack bar?
6. What colour are the lifeguard's shorts?
7. What type of animal is the large inflatable?
8. How many beach umbrellas are there?
9. How many balls are there altogether?
10. What footwear is by the side of the pool?

If you throw a white hat into the Red Sea, what happens?

It gets wet!

If you throw a white stone into the Red Sea, what happens?

It sinks!

PLAY OUTSIDE

You don't have to find a crazy golf course to play
this game – half the fun is making up your own course!

Crazy Golf

The only thing you will need is a ball – a lightweight, plastic one is best. As
for the crazy golf course, find an open area and then use anything to hand.
If you're camping or picnicking: use chairs, baskets, plastic plates, containers,
blankets, twigs and stones for the course. On the beach, make obstacles by
piling up or digging into the sand. For the holes on your golf course, use plastic
cups or small buckets.

Your crazy golf club can be a tennis racket, cricket bat, plastic spade, or even
just a sturdy, straight stick. If a plastic set of clubs is available, wonderful.

When you have created your course of three or four holes, players take it in
turns to go round. The player who takes the fewest shots, wins.

SURF DUDES

Only two of these surfer dudes are exactly the same. Can you spot which two?

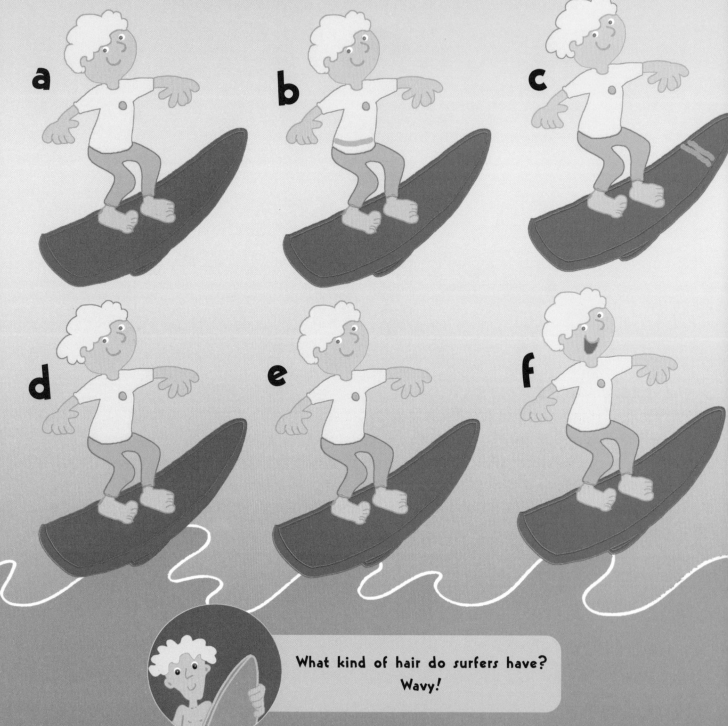

What kind of hair do surfers have?
Wavy!

TEDDY'S WORLD TOUR

Do you take a favourite toy with you on holiday? Why not make sure it's in lots of your holiday snaps? You can stick some here.

A WALK IN THE WOODS

How many things beginning with 'b' can you spot in this picture?

Why do bears
have fur coats?
Because they can't find
hoodies that fit them!

MAKE A WINDMILL

Cut out the square below, then follow the instructions on the next page to make a windmill. You will need a drinking straw, a bead and a split pin.

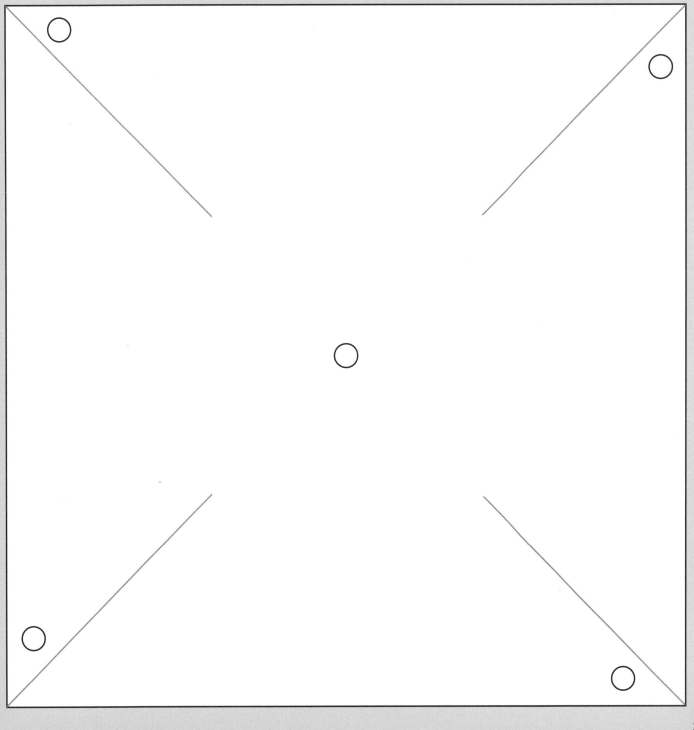

1. Colour both sides of the windmill, then cut along the grey lines. Fold half of each corner into the middle, like this:

2. Ask an adult to help push the split pin through the layers of paper to hold the windmill together.

3. Ask an adult to make a hole near the top of the straw.

4. Push the pin through the straw, add the bead, and fasten the pin.

KITE SURFING

Can you work out which kite surfer is holding on to each kite?
Which kite has come loose?

NIGHT AT THE MUSEUM

What's your favourite thing to see at a museum? Draw it here.

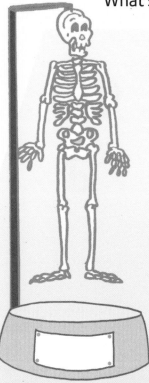

SPoRTs DaY

What are your favourite sports?
Can you find these ten words hidden in the sports grid?

A H R U G B Y Q U E
N S B A S E B A L L
O A B D T E N N F S
T U H A G O L F O Q
N Q O X L L A B Q U
I S C R I C K E T T
M Q K X S O C C E R
D T E N N I S C W N
A B Y Q B A L L Z N
B A S K E T B A L L

BADMINTON   GOLF
BASEBALL   HOCKEY
BASKETBALL   RUGBY
CRICKET   SQUASH
SOCCER   TENNIS

If you have a referee in
football and an umpire in tennis,
what do you have in bowls?
Cereal!

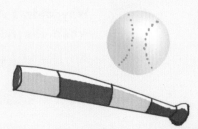

SHARK ATTACK!

Can you find a way through the waves without bumping into any sharks?

Why didn't Mum panic when she fell in the ocean?

All the sharks were man-eaters!

EYES SHUT

Bored of your journey? Fed up of waiting for someone to play in the pool with you? Play this game on your own to pass the time.

Close your eyes and face the window of the car, train or bus you're travelling on. If you're by the pool, just close your eyes.

Now guess what will be the first thing you see when you open your eyes. Count to 10 and then... OPEN!

Did you get it right? Set yourself challenges: instead of just guessing that a person will walk past, see if you can guess whether it will be a grown up or a child, or a man or a woman. If you are certain you're going to see a car, guess whether it will be big or small, or what colour it will be.

Score a point for each correct guess, or five points for a harder challenge if your guess was spot on.

HIDEAWAY

Can you find the small grid of symbols hidden somewhere in the larger grid?

STOP!

This travel game is really easy to learn, but the more you play, the more tactical you become! Play on these boards, then draw your own grids on squared paper.

Two people play this game. Player one draws lines going across (horizontal), player two draws lines going down (vertical).

Player one draws a line anywhere on the board. The line must cover two squares.

Player two draws a line, covering a different pair of squares.

Players keep taking turns until there are no moves left; that is, until a player can't draw a line to cover two squares.

The other player is the winner.

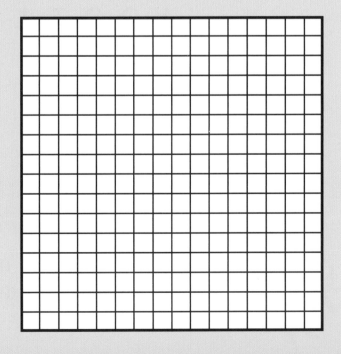

BUG HUNTING

Going on a trip outdoors allows you to see lots of interesting bug life.
Can you find these 10 bugs hidden in the grid?

```
O U S P I D E R L W
S A B E T B U T T O
P N S B E E T L E O
I T L A D Y B I R D
W L U S W A P S D L
A A G E O W S N B O
S D W B R O P A E U
P Y A U M O I I O S
B U T T E R F L Y E
W O O T L A D Y K X
```

ANT   SNAIL
BEETLE   SPIDER
BUTTERFLY   WASP
LADYBIRD   WOODLOUSE
SLUG   WORM

Why did the fly fly?
Because the spider spied her.

48

MAKE A MOSAIC

Colour the pattern to make it as beautiful as possible.

SNOW FUN

Which of these snowboarders is the odd one out?

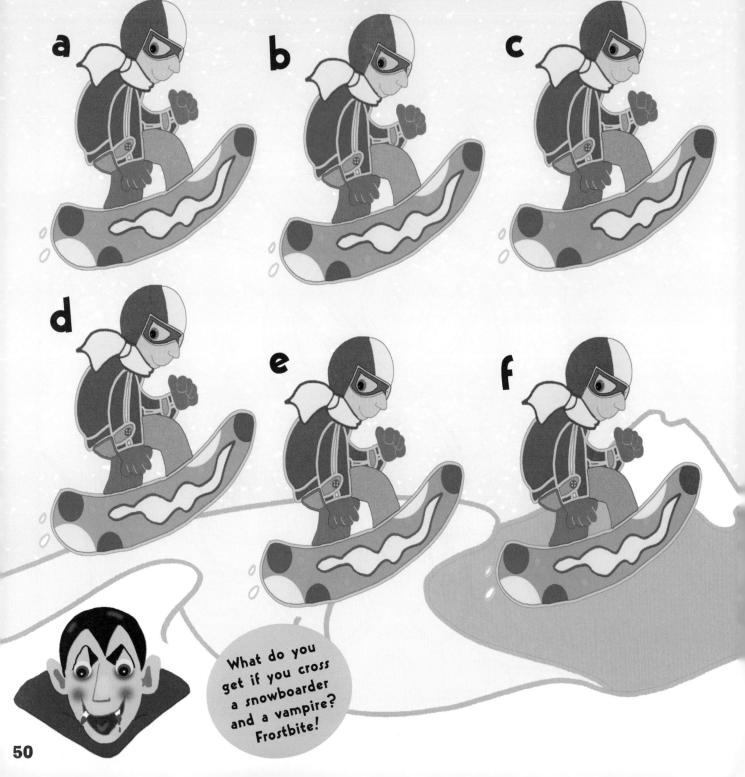

What do you get if you cross a snowboarder and a vampire? Frostbite!

HAPPY DAYS

Use this page to record the best bits of your holidays.

Date: _____

Today I visited: _____

_____

People who came with me:

_____

_____

Stick your ticket here.

Weather: ☐ ☐ ☐ ☐ ☐

Best part: _____

Score: __/10

Other good bits: _____

_____

I ate: _____

I played: _____

_____

Today was:

☐ Simply awesome   ☐ Just brilliant
☐ Good fun   ☐ Quite a laugh
☐ Not bad   ☐ Disappointing

Draw a picture or paste a photo here.

TREASURE SEEKERS

Use an empty sandwich box for collecting 'treasure'.
Can you find each of the items on this list?

- Y-shaped twig
- Leaf with three points
- Ticket
- Acorn or nut
- Smooth stick
- Pink petal
- Stone that is NOT grey
- DIY item such as a screw
- Different kinds of grass
- Sweet wrapper
- Something that begins with the first letter of your name
- Shiny item
- Leaves in two different colours
- Coin
- Receipt

STAY SAFE!
Always tell an adult what you are doing.
Don't wander out of sight of your group.
Don't pick up sharp or dirty rubbish.
Don't harm nature to collect an item.
Wash your hands when you've finished.
Don't leave litter.

GUITAR MAN

Can you help the guitarist through the maze to find the campfire?

PLAY OUTSIDE

Gather a big group of friends together and play this fun game with a difference.

Run Away!

First, you need to mark out the pretend 'river' that you have to cross. Draw lines in the sand, or use string or skipping ropes if you have them.

One person stands in the middle of the river and catches the other players. The others line up along the river bank. They must try to get across to the other river bank without being caught.

Anyone who is caught has to join hands and try to catch other people to make the chain longer.

Remember, the chain of people has to stay inside the river at all times. The last person to be caught is the winner.

COLOUR BY NUMBERS

Follow the colour key to finish this picture.

1 = red
2 = green
3 = yellow
4 = blue

FUN, FUN, FUN!

How many words can you make from the letters below?
Two words are listed to get you started.

HOLIDAYS ARE FUN!

surf

horse

What word begins with t, ends with t,
and has t in the middle?
Teapot!

GOING DOTTY

Two or three players can have great fun with this game. Each player needs a pencil.
Play on this grid, then draw your own on scrap paper.

1 Player one draws a line, straight or curved, between two dots. Draw a new dot on the line, like the example.

2 Player two does the same. Keep taking turns drawing lines and dots.

3 A line isn't allowed to cross or touch another line, and only three lines can extend from a single dot. You can draw a line from one spot back to itself, though.

4 Carry on until no more lines can be drawn. The person who draws the last line is the winner.

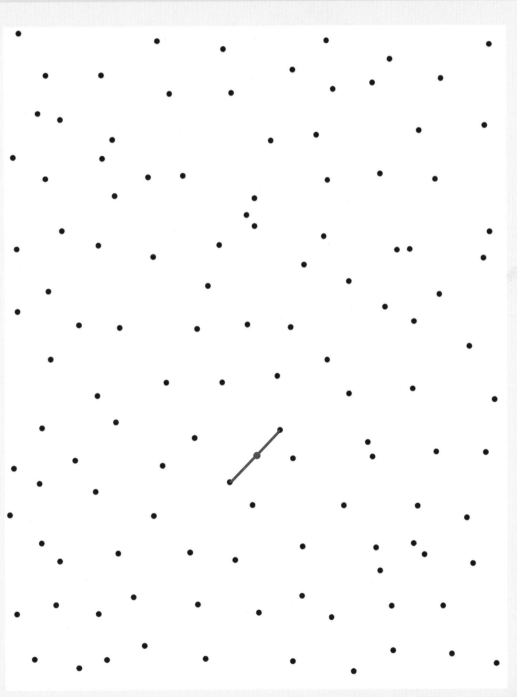

COUNTERS

You can play this game just about anywhere! You need two players, with 13 stones or coins to act as counters.

Put the coins or stones in the middle. Player one picks up one, two or three counters and keeps them.

Player two takes his turn in the same way. Keep taking turns, always picking up one, two or three counters.

When the last counter has been taken, count how many each player has in total. The winner is the player with an even number of coins. It's really easy to play this game, but a lot harder to make sure you win every time!

DOT TO DOT

Join the dots from 1 to 50 to see what the picture is.

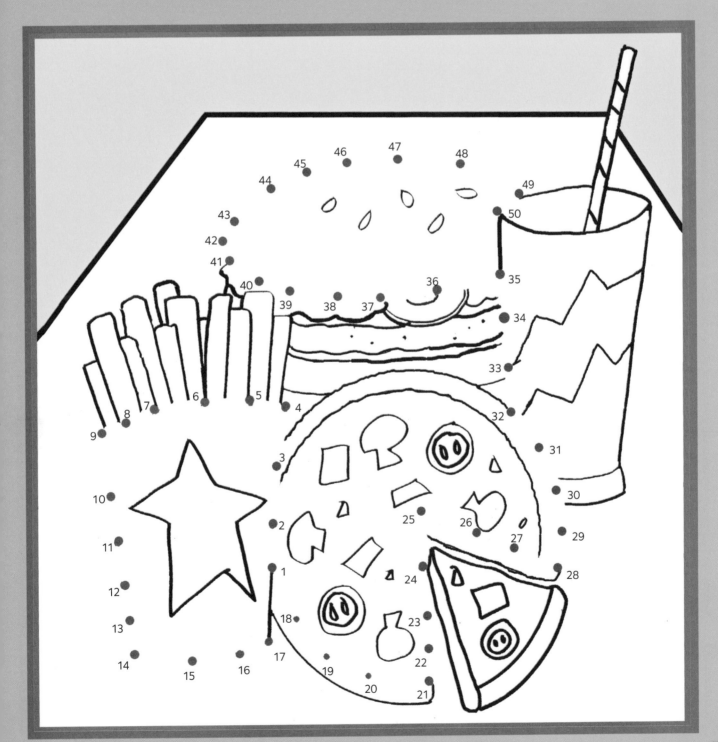

HEADS OR TAILS?

Finish these creatures to make them as realistic or as crazy as you like!

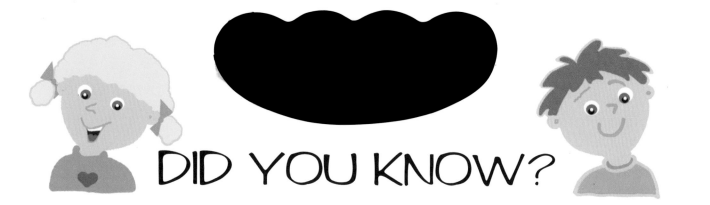

DID YOU KNOW?

Most tornadoes happen after lunch, usually between 2pm and 6pm.

In 2003, a hailstone fell in Nebraska that was 7 inches (18 centimetres) across: that's nearly three times bigger than a tennis ball!

Washington State's Mount Baker Ski Area had 29 metres (95 feet) of snowfall in just one winter!

In 2006, yellow snow fell in Russia. A few weeks later, red snow fell! They were caused by air pollution and sandstorms mixing with the snow.

Earth is struck by lightning an average of 1,000 times every second.

ANSWERS

3 Waterworld

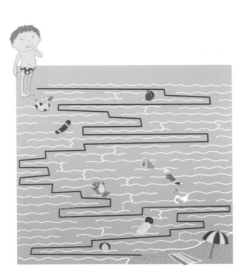

5 Which Sandwich?
Sandwich b

6 Hit the Beach

7 Around the World
RUSSIA

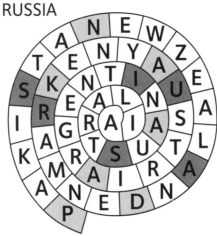

10/11 Brain-busting Quiz

1. c	2. c
3. d	4. b
5. d	6. c
7. a	8. a
9. d	10. c
11. b	12. a

12 Show-stopper

13 Tickets, Please
Tenerife
Istanbul
Amsterdam
Johannesburg
Honolulu

14 Flying High
Kite b flies the highest.

17 On Safari

18 On your Bike
Bike d

19 Lovely Lollies

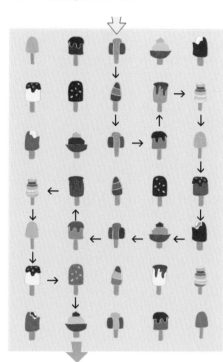

20 I-Spy

22 Treasure Hunt
The treasure is on the beach at A2.

24 Market Maze

25 Chequered Flag

```
H W (H A I R P I N)X
A (C W(W H E E L)D M
M O H D Y K W Z R E
E C E R I N D C S C
C K(P I T S T O P)H
H P I V B E(F M O A
I I N E R E L E I N
C T D(R A L A C L I
(B R A K E S)G H E C
F L(I N D Y C A R)F
```

26/27 Mega Quiz
1.	c	2.	b
3.	c	4.	d
5.	a	6.	c
7.	a	8.	c
9.	b	10.	d
11.	b	12.	a

28 Fruit-oku

29 Jig-fit
Piece d

30 Country Confusion

JAMAICA   GREECE

SWITZERLAND   JAPAN

INDIA   SPAIN

32/33 Memory Test
1. 2 yachts
2. yellow (with a red stripe)

Memory Test (continued)
3. 12:30
4. donkey
5. ice cream, hot dogs
6. red
7. crocodile/alligator
8. 1
9. 7
10. flip flops

36 Surf Dudes
Surfers a and e

38 A Walk in the Woods
Boots, bobble hat, bottle, backpack, bird, boy, binoculars, bushes, book, baseball cap - and don't forget the bear!

41 Kite Surfing
Kite b has come loose.

43 Sports Day

44 Shark Attack!

46 Hideaway
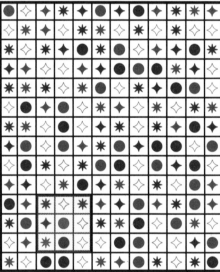

48 Bug Hunting

O U S P I D E R L W
S A B E T B U T T O
P N S B E E T L E O
I T L A D Y B I R D
W L U S W A P S D L
A A G E O W S N B O
S D W B R O P A E U
P Y A U M O I I O S
B U T T E R F L Y E
W O O T L A D Y K X

50 Snow Fun
Snowboarder c

53 Guitar Man

64